Ten Minute Parenting

by

Barbara Hair, M. Ed

Introduction

Parents are the most important people in the world.

There are roles with great responsibility, lucrative careers, world famous performers, Nobel peace prizewinners, powerful and influential people, but none of them are nearly as important as a good parent.

Good parents influence the world, yes the entire world. They make a difference in their homes, neighborhoods, cities and countries. The impact multiplied in the good works, kindness, charity and responsibility they pass onto their children is priceless.

This book is a guide for parents who want to raise strong and responsible children. It is meant to inspire and guide you as you raise your children. It is a common sense, practical guide to bringing up loving, responsible and respectful children.

This book is dedicated to all parents

TABLE OF CONTENTS

Forward

If you do not form your children while they are young, then the outside world will do it for you. You will end up wondering why your children do the things they do or say the things they say when you did not raise them that way.

This book is meant to be a guide for parents who want to raise strong and responsible children. I am writing this to inspire and guide you through the early formations of your children. This is meant to be a guide to help you raise them to be loving, responsible and respectful children.

Parents are the most important factor in the formation of children. What you do and say has life altering effects. It is not by accident that you were entrusted with this young life. In the grand design of life, you were chosen as the perfect parent for your child. They were placed into your arms because you *are* the perfect parent for them. You were chosen to see them through life's trials and tribulations, struggles and successes, problems and resolutions. I hope you find in this guide the support, encouragement and wisdom that you seek.

~How can you count your blessings if you never have any troubles?

RESPECT

Good manners are valued and important. However, the definition of what good manners are varies from parent to parent. You may be thinking that it is too early or too late to teach your child good manners. However, there is no time like the present to begin. So let's start at the beginning and talk about manners.

Manners are the way in which all people interact and treat each other. The way they speak to each other, the way they touch each other and the way that they put out their hand to offer a firm handshake. There is a level of good manners that is impressive and there are several key elements to good manners.

Children who look at people when they are speaking show good manners. Children who greet adults and say hello show good manners. Children who look at people when they are talking show good manners.

Teach your children to say "please" and "thank you". If they make a mistake or hurt someone, teach them to apologize. On the flip side teach them to accept an apology graciously.

In our culture, when someone apologizes the most common response has become, "oh, that's okay". But it is *not* okay or it would not need an apology. If your children make a mistake, let them admit it by extending an apology.

A story to learn from...

One day a mom and her son were at the playground. Everyone was enjoying the afternoon until a playmate took away a toy from the little boy; let us call him Sammy... Screaming ensued and parents intervened. The offender was instructed to apologize to Sammy however Sammy wasn't having any of it! What's a parent to do?
Sammy's mom said, "Sammy is upset and can't accept your apology, so I will accept it for him."
This wise mom knew that good manners must prevail and she was there to help her child.

A family held a gathering at their home for co-workers and as the adults gathered in the living room one of the young sons wandered into the room. His dad proceeded to introduce him to a guest when the boy put out his hand, looked the adult in the eye and said hello. The guest was flabbergasted! Where did the young boy learn such great manners? "At school," the parent replied. That family of course had a great part in the poise and confidence of their sons but it was great to know that some schools teach manners as well.

~Manners matter...

EMOTIONAL BANK ACCOUNT

Children are beautiful and unique human beings. Inside each child is what can be referred to as an emotional bank account. We are not talking about the amount of money you have in your savings account or your 401K. It is your child's *emotional* bank account.

This bank account is built up over time. The balance increases whenever a child receives praise, a thank-you or perhaps an award. These deposits consist of anything that makes them feel good about themselves.

Think about how many times your child receives a deposit into his or her emotional bank account. Be aware of how many times you praise them for what they have done each day. Every time you do this you are making a deposit into their emotional bank account.

There are many ways to make a deposit into their emotional bank account. Take a moment to think about how you commend, praise, reward and show your child love.

As a parent you know your child best. You know the way to touch their heart and how to make them feel loved and appreciated. It doesn't necessarily have to be anything big, perhaps a note in their lunchbox, a little help, a smile or a hug. These little things go into their emotional bank account and they all add up!

When you need to discipline them you are making a withdrawal from their emotional bank account. When the child does not have enough in their account and a withdrawal is made they experience a negative balance. A negative balance is exactly that - a negative state. They begin to feel negative about themselves, the world is bleak and dark, and things just aren't going well for them. It is important for parents to build up the emotional bank account and avoid making a withdrawal before there is enough to cover it.

Another way to think of this is a cup, another image frequently used. Every warm and loving thing you say or do pours into your child's cup. It fills them up, makes them feel important, loved and worthwhile. Ask yourself, "How full is their cup?"

Often times there are children who seem to have a hole in the bottom of their cup. No matter how much praise or effort you might be putting in there never seems to be enough to get it overflowing.

This is one of those situations where you must be patient. Keep trying knowing that sooner or later that it will pay off.

If this describes your child it is extremely important to hang in there. Remember the payoff down the road will definitely be worth it!

Consider the precious moments throughout the day to praise and encourage your children. Look for moments throughout the day when you can catch them being good. Pay attention and reward them. Do not let good behavior go unnoticed!

A story to learn from…

A young mother had finished her shopping, groceries were in the car and the children were all buckled up. Before she started the car she turned around, looked at her children and said, "I am such a lucky mom to have you as my children. I love you." There were big smiles all around!

~Here's my cup, now fill it up!

MEAN IS MY MIDDLE NAME

Raising children is a challenge. Many parents find themselves in situations where their children have them wrapped around their little finger and sometimes the parents don't even realize it. You may be asking yourself, "Is that me?" or you might be saying "that definitely IS me!" Regardless, take this short quiz:

Do you have a firm tone of voice that your children respond to immediately?

Do you have "the look" that stops them dead in their tracks?

Do other parents compliment your child's behavior?

Do other parents ask you, "How do you do it?"

Do your children interrupt your conversations with others?

Effective parents have developed a firm voice that they use when necessary, if you do not have one - practice one. Depending on the situation parents need to be firm and clear. Parents cannot always be sugar and sweetness; they must also be firm and loving.

TIME-OUT

Have you ever heard parents warn their children over and over again they are going to get a time-out? That, of course, is not an effective way to discipline.

Let's look at the key elements of the time-outs. The younger the child is the shorter the time-out. Generally, the rule of thumb is one minute for every year of age. For example, if you have a four-year old who is misbehaving their time-out would last four minutes.

A timer may be helpful because a common mistake is putting a child in time-out and losing track of time. This is not helping your child. This will blur their concept of time and ultimately make those time-outs ineffective. The use of a timer gives the child closure on the misbehavior. When the timer goes off reassure your child that you love them and send them on their way.

Verbal warnings can be an effective tool for parents when disciplining their child. If a child is misbehaving let them know the consequence if they 0continue. Clearly tell them to stop. Be specific. A common mistake is telling a child to "stop it" but the child doesn't know what "it" is.

A story to learn from...

A dad saw his son throwing sand and yelled, "Stop it!" The little boy looked confused as if to say, "Stop what?"

When telling your child to stop doing something be very clear about it. "Honey, if you don't stop hitting Emily you're going to time-out." "If you don't stop yelling there will be a consequence."

If the child continues misbehaving put them in time-out. Remember, you are the adult and they are the child. Help them gently but firmly to their timeout.

Some parents put their child in the nearest corner. (They tell me that they can be found almost anywhere and are handy when you travel.) Some families have a "naughty chair". Find a place that works for you.

Put your child in timeout for "x" amount of minutes and then go set the timer. Make sure your child knows why they are in a timeout. Don't get drawn into a conversation or debate about it.

Many children will pout or cry. Others may sit there seemingly unaffected by the timeout. You may think that it is not having an impact. Rest assured you are being effective. You are teaching your child consistency and consequences.

This is worth repeating. You are teaching your child *consistency and consequences*, two very important lifelong lessons. When the timer goes off say, "Honey, you are finished with your time-out let's go have some fun." Do you remember the old adage, "forgive and forget"? This is one of those times.

A story to learn from...

A mom was disciplining her young daughter and the child yelled, "Mom, you're mean!" Mom replied, "Mean is my middle name."

Sometimes your child will not like you but you will be disciplining out of love. Later you can explain to them that you do what you do because you love them and want the best for them.

~Remember you are your child's parent, not their friend.

TEMPER, TEMPER

It is my hope that the first time that you experience a temper tantrum with your child you are in the privacy of your own home. This will make handling it so much easier for you because a tantrum is a cry for attention and often for the wrong reasons.

As a parent you don't want to give a tantrum any more attention than it deserves. If you can ignore a tantrum that's great because your child will learn that throwing a tantrum is an ineffective way to get your attention or to get something they want.

Some parents have told me that they handle tantrums by looking at their child and saying, "Can't you scream any louder?" Others say, "Keep it up," because they know if they ignore the tantrum and live through the kicking and screaming they will have won a great victory. Not that raising children is meant to be a battle, but you want to avoid a power struggle.

A story to learn from...

A small child picks up the cell phone and tries to make a call. The parent responds, "Johnny, I told you not to play with my phone. You're in time-out." The parent has identified the specific behavior to the child. Way to go so far...
"You are to stay in time-out for four minutes." Next thing you know the parent is sitting there with them talking. Wait a minute, that's not time-out!

A time-out is when the child is away from others and the situation. Time-out means time away from everything. If you send your child to time-out in their room with books, games, toys and things to entertain them, you haven't given them a time-out you've just given them another place to entertain themselves. That's not the message you want to send.

In a time-out there should be no talking, no games and no interaction. (If you want to send your child to their room that's great but just remember it is not a time-out).

Time-out is an effective consequence for misbehavior when implemented consistently and correctly.

Every action has a consequence, good or bad.

Picture this. A small child throws himself down on the ground, screams and cries at the tops of their lungs. This is a temper tantrum, a way of manipulating you and a way for a child to get their way. If you give in they will do it again because they will have triumphed!

Ignore the first temper tantrum. Let your child release all of that energy. Keep your cool, be calm and see it through. When it's over, reassure your child that you love them, hug them and say, "Let's move on". Remember, forgive and forget.

What do you do when your child throws a tantrum in a public place? You must be strong enough and firm enough to take control of the situation. Don't give into your child's tantrum because you feel public pressure to do so. Dealing with a crying child is uncomfortable to handle and uncomfortable for other people to view. Take comfort in the fact that many parents have been in your shoes.

If you give in to a tantrum you are only prolonging the behavior. The best course of action is to tell your child to stop and if they do not then remove them. It takes a strong parent to say, "We're leaving the store now". You may have seen parents leave shopping carts behind, a crying child in tow, heading back to the car. I'm sure that parent takes no great joy in having to do this, but the effect in the long run is worth this uncomfortable spectacle.

We need to support and encourage fellow parents to do the right thing in these types of situations, instead of casting disdaining glances or passing judgment on them. We should support each other by smiling and nodding reassuringly to these parents to show them that we understand their situation and affirm that they are doing the right thing.

~Be Strong!

READY FIRST

It's early in the day and you've got to get to that morning appointment at the dentist's office. One key thing should be first on your mind: you need to be ready first.

It's like when you travel on an airplane and they tell you to please put the oxygen mask on yourself first and then assist your small child. The same plan applies when you're going somewhere with a small child. Make sure that you are ready first.

Keys in hand you are ready to go, now focus on your child and help them to get ready to go. You can give your child a two-minute warning or you can help them get ready. Either way you will have reduced your stress level as well as theirs.

It is important for you to realize that children need time to transition from one activity to another. Just because you are ready to go doesn't mean that they can make that transition as quickly. Give them time, be patient and you will both benefit.

A story to learn from...

It was early in the morning and a mother was getting ready to leave the house with her two children. Her little boy eagerly prepared for the day and mom was ready too. However, her daughter was having a terrible time getting out of bed. Rather than getting mad this mother went in, took the child in her arms, held her, soothed her and shared a precious moment. This one minute of love and reassurance was enough to help that little girl get out of bed. Lesson learned; one moment of love can change the course of the day.

Let's say you're at the playground and you need to send a signal to your child that it is time to go. Again, you're ready first and you are set to go. Don't be the parent that says you're ready to go and then continue to talk to someone for another ten minutes.

Think about this for a minute. When you tell them that you are ready to go, be ready to go. Say what you mean and mean what you say.

How do you help your children come away from the playground? You may have observed that teachers or playground monitors have a signal. Some tools include a whistle, a hand-clap or that recognizable signal your children know that will get their attention.

When your children do as they are told, show your joy and reward them for their prompt obedience. Remember that emotional bank account? Good!

~Put your oxygen mask on yourself first before assisting your child.

NO!

No other word in the English language is stronger or more powerful than the word "no". Yet this small two-lettered word holds such great weight with people.

What does the word "no" really mean to a child? "May I go play with my friends?" If your response is "no", the "no" is restrictive. "May I have a piece of cake?" When you say "no" then that's a denial of pleasure.

There are so many ways "no" translates into meaning for a child. Adults also have a different interpretation for the word "no". When my daughter was two-years old is seemed that the only word she knew was "no". Did I use that word so often that she picked it up so quickly? Was that my intention?

One of the words that "no" had come to replace is "stop". For example, when a child is doing something that could be dangerous or could lead to injury, it is instinctive to yell "no!" instead, say "stop!"

Young mothers need to practice when to say "no" to their children. Some children seldom hear the word "no" or have never been told the word "no".

Practice Makes Perfect.

Even though you could be saying yes to a request from your child, they need to learn the concept. A simple example is if your child asks for a drink of juice. You could say yes because the juice is there. However, you take this opportunity to teach your child the word "no". In this instance I choose to say "no". They may cry and scream but that is part of the lesson that "no" means "no". Repeat this throughout the early years of your child's development.

The underlying lesson is that not everything in life is a "yes". They will need to deal with and learn the many disappointments throughout their life. "No" is a lesson in life.

A story to learn from…

Here is a technique you may find effective. After saying "no" look your child in the eye and ask them, "Are you going to cry now?" If you try this technique often enough your child will learn that crying and whining will not work on you and they will stop. This will give you the satisfaction of knowing that they have learned this lesson.

One way to eliminate your use of the word no is to offer your child choices. A wise parent will not allow unlimited requests. For example, at snack time do not ask, "What would you like for snack?" This opens the door to an inexhaustible list of things that are on the "no" list. Instead say, "Would you like apples or carrot sticks?" If the child begins to ask for other things tell them those are not choices and repeat, "Would you like apples or carrot sticks?" If you are consistent they will quickly learn that you say what you mean and mean what you say.

~Set limits!

MAKING MISTAKES AND FORGIVENESS

Because we're all human, we all make mistakes. For children it's important for them to learn how to deal with them. We don't want our children growing up thinking that they don't make mistakes, or that making a mistake makes them bad or stupid. The response that we have is very important and so are the lessons that we teach them at a young age.

There are many different kinds of mistakes. The focus of this chapter is not on what kinds of mistakes are made, but how to handle them. We need to teach our children how to apologize and how to admit to a mistake. This will teach them the virtue of humility as well.

When you're dealing with a young child make sure that there is an ending to a mistake whether it is a time-out, a consequence, or short conversation. Avoid making this a sermon or a lecture. There also needs to be some kind of acknowledgement or an apology.

Consider when one child hurts the feelings of another child. In this situation, take your child aside and let them know that "we don't use those words" or "we don't talk to someone like that and you need to apologize". If you use consistent language your child will learn to apologize without too much prodding.

Keep each apology very simple, short and concise. Explain the need to say, "I'm sorry I hurt your feelings".

The other half of this lesson is teaching your children how to accept an apology. In our culture today we have taught children to say, "Oh, that's okay" when in fact it is *not* okay. Teach your children to say, "Apology accepted". This is for the benefit of both children involved. It brings closure to the situation.

Do not allow your child to refuse or rebuke an apology. If at the moment they are too emotional to do it themselves, then you need to step in, turn to the other child and say, "Johnny is not ready to accept your apology right now, but I will accept it for him". Thank the child for apologizing.

There are several reasons for this. First, you are acknowledging your child's emotional state. Second, you are giving closure to the situation with the offending child. Third, you're modeling the correct behavior for your child.

~Learn to forgive...

ROUTINE AND DISCIPLINE

Children need routine. There is no way to get around it. For those of you who embrace this idea, you probably already have a plan of action in place and routine seems to come more naturally. You have things organized in your home. You have a set bedtime for your children. You have a set morning routine where the breakfast is ready and backpacks are by the door. You have keys that go in one basket and things are in their place. You are very successful in your routine and should commend yourselves for this achievement. You've streamlined your home and things are running smoothly.

However, in this chapter, let's focus on those who are yearning for this organization and routine.

For some reason temperament, personality or the way we were raised prevents us from developing good habits. We're the ones who buy the self-help books or cry out to others to please "Help me!" We have every intention of being organized or being on schedule but this remains a constant struggle. If fact, there are those of us who need more than an occasional tune-up, we need a full overhaul.

Routine is important. Here are just a few tips that may help you. When it comes to children, it is good to give them time to transition. When you say, "We need to leave now", you're sending a signal to your children that you mean immediately– you said now. If you don't leave right then, you're sending a mixed signal to them that you're not serious. Set an example. You need to stay focused if you expect them to be focused as well. It is so important for parents to give their children a verbal warning, especially young children, because they really don't have a firm grasp of time.

No one wants to be surprised by an unexpected event or be rushed out the door. Once children become involved in a book, a game or a show they need time to transition away from them. Parents need to give children a warning: two-minute or five-minute warning. Set a timer if you need it. Then when the timer sounds you have to be ready yourself and your children know that they should be ready.

If you are consistent your children will learn this routine as well as two important lessons. First, you mean what you say, and second, two minutes passes quickly.

I respect a parent's right to discipline their child. However, anything in excess is not good. This applies to physical or verbal punishment. Verbal punishment such as belittling can be very detrimental. So we want to leave that out of the picture altogether.

We want consistency, love and clear expectations to be the foundation for loving discipline. These elements are so important I cannot emphasize them enough.

Clear expectations are *very* important. I have seen several great examples when parents communicate their expectations with a child.

Here is an example. A young mother had several small children who were going to visit an elderly relative named Aunt Geri. When they arrived the mother got the children together, bent down on her knees to be at eye level with her children, looked them in the eye and proceeded to tell them what her expectations were during their brief visit. She told them to walk in quietly, sit down on the sofa and listen politely. She also said that if they were good during their visit they would earn a treat.

These small children understood what was expected of them, they knew it wasn't going to be forever and their mom knew they could to be polite and quiet. When they walked into the home the children knew what was expected of them. Aunt Geri was amazed! The children went in and did exactly what was expected of them because their mom had been clear in her communication with them. Those children didn't need to ask questions because the mother was clear and concise in her expectations.

Meal time can be an area where parent expectations may need adjustment. Do not give your child too much food on their plate and expect them to eat it all. A wise parent will serve children small portions, first reassuring them that if they eat what's on their plate they can always ask for more. This not only eliminates waste but also gives children the opportunity to say "please" and "thank you."

A story to learn from...

It's five o'clock and everything is falling apart! The children are cranky, the dog is underfoot, the work day is over and nerves are frazzled... how can this be? Wise parents know that for some unknown reason this part of the day "is what it is" and there may be no getting around it.

Nothing in this world is perfect and there are going to be times when no matter what you do things are rough. Think of this as the power hour and a normal transition into the closing of the day. Remember, you must weather the storm to reach calm waters.

Parents make the mistake of telling their children that "I want you to be good" or "I want you to behave" but children do not really understand exactly what is expected. What does "be good" mean? Parents, make your expectations clear. For instance, when you are going to introduce your child to someone, tell your children to look that person in the eye, shake his or her hand and say "Hello". In this way you will be clearly communicating your expectations to your child.

~Make expectations clear.

JOY

You may be wondering why there is a chapter like this in a book for parents. I feel that it is very important to remind you that your children are a joy! They are a gift to you.

A large part of raising a child should include moments of playfulness and joy. So many times parents say to me, "There's just not enough time in the day". Or perhaps, "I'm so rushed and stressed". Many of us lead very busy lives and juggling a job, home and family is quite a challenge.

However, when you look at the bigger picture, you'll want to make sure that you have set aside times, not just for vacations, but small moments that your children will cherish.

Let me give you an example. You may have memories of when you and your child were on a great vacation. Ask them to tell you something that was a special memory to them. Their response may surprise you. Children will mention things like playing cards or playing a game. Those were the moments when all you did was simply spend time together.

So I would like to encourage you to all be mindful of these moments. Try to remember each day, or as often as you can, to set aside time for the "joyful moment". It might be the moment that comes unexpectedly when you have just one or two minutes.

These types of moments happen often in a child's life but are frequently overlooked. Parents quite literally "overlook" them. Children are small and adults are tall; when little children share a giggle of excitement, jump for joy or share that really wacky, silly comment - parents literally don't hear them and look right over them.

Make a new resolution today. Look for joyful moments by getting down to your child's eye level or lift them up to your level. Whatever you do live in the moment! It's those little gifts that mean so much and I cannot emphasize it enough how important even a minute can be to a child.

Having you look into their eyes and for them to know that you are really listening is the greatest gift that you could give your child. You are strengthening the bond between you and your child, a bond that will be tested throughout the years.

~Keep your sense of humor.

HOMEWORK

Parents often have questions about whether they should help their child with homework. How much help should I give my child? What is my role? I would like to clarify these questions for you.

First of all, homework should be a review of the things that the child has already covered in class. Most students should feel that the material is a review. The only exception would be a special project or book report unique to the child. Let's begin with the youngest of children.

Kindergarten is an important environment in which to develop good study habits and social skills. The best early childhood educators know that kindergarten children must develop a positive attitude towards homework. It should be enjoyable yet focused.

School newsletters recommend that parents provide a quiet place for their children to do homework. It should be a consistent place, such as the kitchen table.

Eliminate as many distractions as possible, such as the television. Children whose parents have actually done this prove to do well in school. Parents who do this are setting their children up for success.

When you turn off the television they may balk at you at first and say that they can do both study and watch TV. Remember, when it really comes down to it you are the parent, you are in control and you set the rules. Eliminate distractions and have your children work for ten minutes and then take a break.

There are some instances when a child will sit at their homework, you leave the room and when you come back to check on their progress they have very little to show for the time elapsed. The question is then how are they using their time?

Obviously, in this case, not very well or they just didn't know what to do. As a parent you need to step in and help them. Again, set the timer for ten minutes. You may need to coach them or even sit down next to them. This is a way for you to help them form good study habits.

As your child grows older you should be able to step away and leave them to do their work for a short amount of time independently.

Proper preparation for homework is vital. It is very frustrating to sit down to do homework only to find you don't have the right tools. Have all materials in one place. Better to be prepared so you're not always running around looking for a ruler or glue stick when you need it.

Recommended items are: crayons, scissors, glue stick, ruler, pens, paper, pencils and a pencil sharpener. These may be small things, but they add up to big things.

It is important to set your child up for success. As they get older, the other tools you may want to have on hand included an atlas, calculator and a good dictionary. Developing a good homework routine will benefit both you and your child.

Another obstacle with homework is trying to figure out how much help you should give them. It's interesting that I often meet parents where the child seems to work better with either the mother or the father. Somehow, whether based on temperament or approaches to a particular subject, one partner or the other seems to be easier for the child to take direction from or simply to work with. This shouldn't be in any way an indication that you are not a good parent.

If you just happen to have an approach that doesn't quite help your child, it takes a humble parent to admit that they are not the best one to help with math. Or perhaps it's time for dad to step in and read the story. Work this out early to avoid a prolonged homework episode.

The more that you struggle on homework with your child the more negative the experience will become. That is something that teachers, parents and students want to avoid. So if you find yourself in difficulty, step back, do a bit of self-evaluating or self-reflection.

Do not be afraid to go to your child's teacher. Whether it's a phone call to the school, writing them a note or sending them an email, keep that communication open. Teachers know your children, but not as well as you do because you live with them and are raising them. It's good to remember that they have insights into educational approaches that you could find very valuable.

Let's do a quick review. Your children need to have a routine: a predictable pattern of homework, where they will be doing it, how much time it's going to take and how you're going to help them. You will have the necessary supplies on hand as well.

As your child grows and changes so will your role in the area of homework. Parents need to reflect and ask themselves, "What is best for my child and what works well for them?" Some students are naturally more independent or they want to do their work by themselves from the very beginning of school. Others will take several years of supervision, which means checking their homework, reminding them and so on. Of course we know that in the long run your children will grow up to be independent people.

When they are young it is often difficult to see that far down the road. But time and time again my experience shows that different styles, different personalities still grow up to become very successful. Parents, please listen to your instincts. Sometimes you may feel swayed by different people or certain events.

Take the time to self-reflect again and ask yourself then what works best for my family. What kind of schedule works well for my child? Do this and it will all work out just fine.

~Trust your instincts!

PARENTING ALONE

This chapter is titled 'parenting alone' for good reason. I had planned on doing a chapter on single parenting for those parents who are divorced, separated or single. However, there are others who are parenting alone because their spouse is away for a variety of reasons. For this group of parents, and for those who are parenting alone, they face very special and unique problems.

The first and foremost question to those parents is: how do you raise a child by yourself? This is the most demanding circumstance because you find yourself running a household and dealing with your child or children exclusively.

You need to develop a support system around you. Choose a school or a daycare that reinforces the manners, expectations and the positive discipline that you employ at home. One of the most destructive things can be if the home and school are not in sync. This causes frustration not only for parents but for the children as well.

There is one exception. There are those children who are so adaptable that they learn the expectations in each of these environments and they work it to their advantage. This means that if the home is structured, very strict and has a specific set of rules they will learn to abide by those rules and they'll adapt in order to follow them. If the school has a different set of rules and a different level of expectations, they will learn these too. But younger children, by and large, do not learn this and that's the hard part. They struggle to live in two different worlds and lack the consistency.

A major obstacle to a single parent is the feeling of guilt. This is a natural feeling. People feel guilty about a number of things in their lives. But as a parent we can't harbor those feelings and we can't let them keep us from being an effective parent.

Also, a trap that some fall into is that they let that guilt lead them into behaviors that are too permissive or not in the best interest of the children. It is important to acknowledge your feelings but then know and accept them and move on.

Many mothers in our culture find themselves alone even when they are in long term and stable marriages. So the next emotion of inadequacy is probably more common than you can imagine. Parenting alone can leave you exhausted and feeling inadequate. You need to find time for yourself and do some self-care. If you do your job and form your children you will have that time. Be sure to build that time into your day.

Be reassured that by parenting alone you *are* adequate. You are your child's parent. You have been given the role of parent not just for the benefit of your child but to the enhancement of your life as well.

When a parent came to me and asked why she was having so many problems with her young son I reassured her that there was a bigger picture to consider. In the grand design of life she was the perfect mom to help him throughout his life. You are there with a major purpose and you can do it!

You can learn to be an effective parent. As a parent, try to create a predictable and stable home. Try to keep job changes to a minimum and keep things more routine in your life. If this is not possible build stability in things that are familiar to your child, such as his or her bedroom or favorite toys. Keeping the essence of familiarity or stability in their lives is very important.

Look around and see who you have in your life to call upon for support. Step forward and ask, "Would you be an adult figure for my child?" or "Would you please carpool with me?" Not being able to ask can be a major stumbling block for a parent. Many people find it difficult to reach out and will not ask for help, they therefore end up doing everything.

A story to learn from…

One day someone came to me and asked if we could carpool. I was happy to help and shared my enthusiasm. She was surprised by my reaction. How can we form loving, compassionate and generous children if we never give them the opportunity to practice these virtues? Adults also need to feel needed. Take a risk and ask for help.

~Let confidence be your friend.

SERVICE

Service is another important part of parenting. Maybe you're thinking, yes, you are a parent, thus a servant, and I am always serving my children. This chapter focuses on community service and service to others. How do you get your children to look beyond themselves or to look beyond their own needs? Some of the best examples of this are families that have several children who are given the opportunity to serve each other at home.

Let's start with the preschoolers. You many think that they are too young to do community service. You're right. You wouldn't want to take them to the soup kitchen or take them to the food bank to sort cans.

49

However, there are small ways for small children to give back. A few examples are to have them go through their toys, sort and donate them to charity. Another would be to do small chores around the house earning coins for a local charity or your church.

Older children are able to help at a school festival, collect food donations and help take them to a food bank. Often it is a school or church group that is a driving force to recruit volunteers. Take a moment and think about places in your community where you as a family can go to serve.

This chapter really came about because I experienced a family that was unfamiliar with community service and did not know how to serve. The children weren't exposed to the larger urban community and they thought that everybody lived in a house; everyone owned a car and everyone had all their needs met.

So when their children made it clear to these parents that they did not realize that there were less fortunate people in the community, the parents realized that it was time for them to step up and make their children aware of the needs of other people.

In larger cities there are shelters, food banks, and churches for people to come and serve. Choose an area of community volunteering and get involved. Don't go alone, but take the hand of your child and try it once. You'll be pleasantly surprised at the impact that first opportunity has on your child. Then as they grow older you'll be open to more opportunities and experiences that will broaden your mind as well as theirs.

Be open to going with them as a co-worker or as support. You are the primary educator for your child. You are the leader.

It is important to teach them to serve. So many times schools take on this responsibility but it is ultimately *you* that sets the example. You will not only be surprised that your child will grow from this experience but that you too will grow as a person as well.

~Serving others is rewarding.

WORDS OF WISDOM

~Don't give your child everything or they will appreciate nothing

~ You can be proud of your children when they are respectful and kind

WORDS OF PRAISE

Good Job

I love you

You're special

Thank you for offering

I appreciate your effort

That was very kind of you to say

Nice try

Good effort

Way to go

There's always next time

What would I do without you?

You look great

You are a blessing from heaven

About the Author

Barbara Hair is a freelance writer, author and private tutor with over thirty years of classroom teaching experience. Ms. Hair earned her Bachelors of Arts in Education through Washington State University and Master's Degree in Education from San Francisco State University. She holds a Washington State Teaching Certificate with an emphasis in elementary and early childhood education. Throughout her years of teaching Ms. Hair has presented a variety of workshops for parents and educators. And, most importantly, she too is a parent.